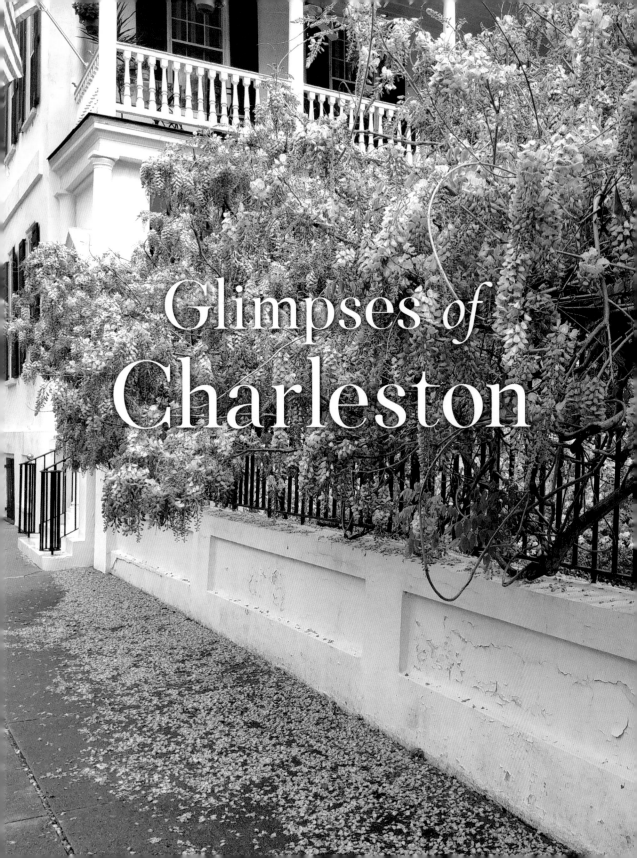

Glimpses of
Charleston

Glimpses *of*
Charleston

DAVID R. AvRUTICK

Globe
Pequot
Guilford, Connecticut

Globe
Pequot

An imprint of The Rowman & Littlefield Publishing
Group, Inc.
4501 Forbes Blvd., Ste. 200
Lanham, MD 20706
www.rowman.com

Distributed by NATIONAL BOOK NETWORK

British Library Cataloguing in Publication Information available

**Library of Congress Cataloging-in-Publication Data
available**

ISBN 978-1-4930-3753-7 (hardcover)
ISBN 978-1-4930-3754-4 (e-book)

∞™ The paper used in this publication meets the
minimum requirements of American National
Standard for Information Sciences–Permanence
of Paper for Printed Library Materials, ANSI/NISO
Z39.48-1992

Printed in the United States of America

To my daughter, Morgan, whose idea planted the seed that blossomed into Glimpses; my son, Ben, whose fastball gets scarier to catch every day; and my wife, Kay, whose deep love for Charleston brought it all together.

Contents

Foreword

I was lucky to be born in Charleston and have lived here my entire life. Still, each day as I walk about this historic and enchanting city I am surprised by its beauty and detail. From the blooming flower boxes, to the colorful stucco, from the aging stone, to the crawling vines covering gates and walls, each glimpse down its streets and alleys hold limitless appeal. How these details come together are not only inspiring, but nourishing to the spirit. It is one of the many reasons Charleston is so desirable to live in and visit.

David has found a way to capture this appeal in his book, *Glimpses of Charleston*. Each page represents David's love for our dear city. I know his love for Charleston runs deep, as I have had the great pleasure of knowing and working with him and his wife Kay over the years, and in 1999, even performed their wedding ceremony at our historic city hall. They and their children, Morgan and Ben, are our neighbors. And it is so wonderful to see their family flourish here in our city.

David's interest in taking photos of Charleston's appeal on his cell phone has now turned into a passion project that is shared on these pages. For Charlestonians, visitors, or those who hope to one day visit, this book is a treasure. It reveals how captivating this city truly is and why so many people fall deeply in love with it, whether they've visited once, or like me, have spent the past seventy-five years here.

–Joseph P. Riley Jr.
Mayor of Charleston from 1975–2016

Introduction:
The Story of Glimpses

I first visited Charleston in 1989 with my then girlfriend, now wife (who is a Charleston native). It was a month after Hurricane Hugo had roared ashore and wreaked havoc on the city and the surrounding Lowcountry of South Carolina. Despite the destruction, I was struck by the incredible beauty and history of the area. What was even more notable was how the residents felt about the city–they just oozed love and passion. They could not stop talking about how much they loved their home and how it so strongly defined who they were.

I've now lived and worked in downtown Charleston for nearly twenty years, having discovered the truth of the saying that "if you marry a girl from Charleston, you'd better pack your bags." I must admit that the city has worked its magic on me, too. While a native might still consider me as being from "off" (the term used for those not born on the Charleston peninsula), I am now tied to this beautiful city and very much feel like a local. My children were born here, and it is our family's home.

As many times as you might visit Charleston (and I certainly came often in the ten years between my first venture and the day I moved here), living here is very different. The beauty and history just seep into your soul and become part of you. With the passion of a recent convert, I wanted to share this feeling with others. I began using my cell phone to photograph some of the sights, details, and beauty that caught my eye, and then I posted the photos on my personal Facebook page.

On a chilly January day in 2013, our daughter, Morgan, said, "Dad, you take such great photos. Why don't you create a page and share them that way?" Thus, *Glimpses of Charleston* was born. The online following grew tremendously and continues to do so not just on Facebook, but on other forms of social media and the Glimpses of Charleston website as well. In each case, the photos and commentary were, and are, offered with my "local's-eye view."

While the Internet is a wonderful and dynamic place to share the beauty of Charleston, having grown up in a family of authors and from working at a large New York publishing house, I always looked forward to creating a tangible *Glimpses* book. It always seemed like a natural thing to do.

I hope some of my love for and perspective of Charleston come through on these pages and that you enjoy this local's-eye view.

Iconic Charleston

With the popularity of Charleston booming (Really, how often can you be named the best city in the universe?), the sites and sights that attract everyone have become more and more familiar and increasingly well known. Movies and TV shows are now often filmed here ("Did you hear who is in town this week?"), and the city is so frequently featured in magazines, books, and websites that all the attention is now greeted with a shrug– or sometimes a wince. The world has embraced Charleston. Rainbow Row, the steeples of St. Michael's and St. Philip's, and the City Market (or Centre Market) are all so beautiful and filled with history, it's easy to see why they attract a lot of attention.

Even for locals, no matter how many times you have seen it, there is a prideful pleasure in viewing the High Battery lit by the morning sun. There is a palatable sense of history when mailing a letter at the post office at the Four Corners of Law, running across the street into City Hall, or viewing the fantastic County Courthouse, just another spot in Charleston that George Washington visited. There is a real appreciation of the vibrancy felt when walking up King Street (even in the face of a tide of visitors) to get to a favorite store or restaurant. As much as we may complain about being stuck in traffic behind a horse-drawn carriage, it's actually a unique way to have a traffic jam (as long as the "equine sanitation" crew also quickly shows up to do its job).

The real beauty of Charleston is, of course, a collective one. It's derived from not just the individual spots that top all the "must-see" lists but from the incredible volume of spectacular houses and buildings, their architectural details, the history that took place in the buildings, the natural environment that surrounds the city, and, perhaps most importantly, the passion with which it is all cherished and protected by the city's residents.

But the must-see sites are mandatory for a reason. You just don't want to miss them. And, of course, that's what makes them iconic.

22   Glimpses of Charleston

28   Glimpses of Charleston

Water, Water Everywhere

By definition, being on a peninsula means that Charleston is bound by water on three sides. In reality, it feels like there is much more than that. With the majestic Ashley and Cooper Rivers, the wonderfully vibrant harbor, and the ocean beyond, water has defined this city since it was first settled, long before the Europeans arrived.

The port is one of the largest drivers of the Charleston economy, receiving shipments from and sending goods (lots of BMWs!) to the rest of the world. Huge container ships share the space with sailing regattas and pods of dolphins. Massive private yachts dock at the City Marina, leading to speculation by those eating at the Marina Variety Store Restaurant (my family's favorite breakfast spot) about their ownership.

With all the water around the city, it's not surprising that it creates some challenges, mainly, how to get over it. While there is a great water taxi between Charleston and Mount Pleasant, and many people own boats, it's the bridges that govern our day-to-day transit. The most famous of them all, the Arthur Ravenel Jr. Bridge, is one of the longest cable-stayed bridges in the world and replaced two Cooper River bridges–the Grace Memorial and the Pearman Bridges. Besides being really striking, it has a fantastic pedestrian/bike lane, which allows for a more intimate use. Bikers, cross-country runners, and back-packers preparing to hike the Appalachian Trail, along with loads of walkers and joggers, train on it as it is one of the only "hills" in the Lowcountry. The bridge is a great spot to catch a panoramic view of the city, the harbor, the rivers, and the barrier islands–all the way out to the Atlantic Ocean. Oh, and it's quite a memorable drive when crossing it, as well

Whether you are crossing a bridge, paddling a dragon boat (very cool), or a kayak (also cool), heading out for a day of fishing, or just strolling along the High or Low Battery, you will find daily life in Charleston subtly, and sometimes not so subtly, shaped by the waters that surround it.

Charleston Houses

Just about the first thing anyone thinks of when they are talking about Charleston are the beautiful houses. The sheer number is staggering. Everywhere you go, particularly in the Historic District, there is one amazing structure after another. It's not surprising that the first historic preservation ordinance in the country was passed in Charleston. The residents' love and reverence for the houses permeate life in the city.

The history of the United States is reflected in so many of the houses, from precolonial times, through the American Revolution and Civil War, to the present day. Many have served multiple roles as military headquarters during conflicts, as hospitals or jails, as boardinghouses or hotels. Although some have become museums or inns and others might be someone's second or third house, the majority are primary residences.

Many of the houses are passed down through the families from generation to generation. With others, different people and families become the "temporary" custodians. We often laugh about how the house owns the people and not vice versa. When taking on the responsibility of owning a Charleston house, not only do you become its current caretaker, you also treasure its history and protect its future.

When we first moved into our downtown Charleston house, I remarked that it felt like we were living in a Norman Rockwell painting. The clip-clop of horses' hooves, whether from the mounted police that existed at that time or a tourist carriage going by, immediately conjured images of earlier times. Sitting in rocking chairs on our porch while sipping iced tea tied us to the generations who came before us. Children still ride their bikes and play in the streets, and neighbors wave as they go in and out of their front doors. The intersection of our street is referred to as "casserole corner," as it is a gathering spot for the families who live here. We raise our children together and share life's milestones, both the good and the bad. While the exteriors of the houses in Charleston are spectacular and wonderful to view, it's what goes on inside that makes them our homes.

Charleston is not just a museum of amazing houses and a library of historical tales, it is truly a living city.

Blooming Charleston

Without a doubt, Charleston is known for its architecture; that beauty is accented and amplified by the innate splendor of the Lowcountry and the city's wonderful gardens, which have been created with vast amounts of love and effort.

The natural setting of Charleston is full of palmetto trees, which adorn the famous state flag, ever-changing marshes, and spectacular live oak trees, all of which act as a casually ornate frame around the city. (Do you know about the Angel Oak in Angel Oak Park? At between 400 and 500 years old, it is thought to be the oldest tree east of the Mississippi.) The man-made gardens and parks, along with the urban forest of tree-lined streets, accent the built city and infuse it with even more color and life. Bird and animal life is abundant, even within the densest parts of downtown. Lizards roam the walls and vines, and all kinds of birds, from the Carolina wren (the state bird) to bald eagles, Cooper's hawks, hummingbirds, egrets, and brown pelicans, are just about everywhere. I once even came face-to-face with a fox trotting down the street while I was out for an early morning run.

The vast array of colors added to the city by the blossoms and flowers is also breathtaking. With its subtropical climate, there is something blooming just about any time of year. Simply walking along the street can take you through a kaleidoscope of color. With many of the houses built right up to the sidewalk, window boxes often take the place of a front yard. Charleston's window boxes are tended to with as much love and effort as many of its famous gardens.

When we first moved into our house, we were so excited by the possibilities of the garden that we got to work on it right away, before we did anything else. Once it was complete, the garden made the outside of the house look so good that we began getting calls from the Historic Charleston Foundation, asking if they could include the house in their annual Tour of Homes. We politely declined, having to confess that the rooms were barely furnished!

Taken together with the architecture, the entire palette of Charleston's beauty embraces you and doesn't let go. It infuses your life and becomes the norm. When I visit other cities, they always remind me of what a special place I get to call home. When artist Alfred Hutty first came to Charleston in 1919, he wrote his wife, "Come quickly, have found heaven." That still sounds just about right.

Holiday Charleston

Charleston loves holidays. Not just Christmas and Hanukkah, where it dresses up elegantly and festively, but also Halloween, Thanksgiving, the Fourth of July, and more. These holidays are all reasons to decorate and celebrate.

Halloween is one of my favorites. Trick-or-treating is a massive event in our neighborhood. We have hundreds of costumed children come to our door each year. Our neighborhood overflows with ghosts (well, we have those year-round), witches, Power Rangers, gorillas, princesses, and fairies. The grown-ups may come dressed up as well, carrying wine glasses that they hope to have refilled at each of their friends' houses. Our first year in the neighborhood, we had bought five or six bags of candy, which we expected to be plenty, and had no alcohol on hand. We quickly ran out of candy and horrified the parents looking for wine.

With that, a new family tradition was born. Each year my wife buys tremendous quantities of candy, makes various types of chili, and lays out a lot of wine, beer, and other beverages. We fling open the doors, and friends and family stop by to eat, drink, and join us on the porch in handing out candy. It's a wonderful time of food and a lot of fun.

When the candy and wine have run out—which is always surprising—we close the gate and turn off the porch lights, signaling an end to the night. This happens up and down the street, all at about the same time. At that point an eerie sugar-filled calm descends. The next morning, we compare with our neighbors how many bags of candy we went through and share our favorite stories from the night before.

A favorite story of mine was once when the trick-or-treating was wrapping up, our candy supply had run down, and the usual wide selection had dwindled. One young man, dressed as a vampire, came up to our porch and very politely said, "Trick or treat." As we were looking to shut things down, I just held out the bowl so he could take what he wanted. After carefully perusing our offerings, he looked up and, again very politely, said, "No, thanks," and went back down the stairs. It was very humbling.

Another of my favorite holidays is Thanksgiving. This is a more formal affair in our Charleston home. My wife loves to pull out the fancy French linens; set our formal dining room with the good china, crystal, and silver; and gather our family and friends. She cooks up a storm, using many family recipes, alongside her piles of Charleston cookbooks. A real Charleston flair that we have added is having local oysters delivered that morning and serving them freshly shucked (by me), on the front porch, along with champagne and plenty of lemon and homemade cocktail sauce.

Whatever the holiday, Charleston can be counted on to celebrate it, and celebrate it all out.

54 TRADD STREET
THE
WILLIAM VANDERHORST
HOUSE
(POSTMASTER BACOT HOUSE)
circa 1740

Constructed circa 1740 by
William Vanderhorst, this three story
stuccoed masonry structure is considered
one of the earliest examples of a
Charleston single house. A notable
aspect of the building is the absence of a
piazza, a development found in single
houses of a later period.

Distinguished residents of 54 Tradd Street
include Mr. Thomas W. Bacot, Charleston's
fifth postmaster and Mr. Abram Sasportas,
one of Charleston's early leading merchants.
The house was restored in the 1920s by
Miss Susan Pringle Frost, founder of the
Preservation Society of Charleston.

placed by
THE PRESERVATION SOCIETY OF CHARLESTON
1982

Stormy Charleston

Living in Charleston brings with it a lot of varied weather. Being subtropical and on the coast, warm weather, wind, and rain are all par for the course. Hurricanes are occasionally expected (but always unwelcome).

Snow, however, isn't something you expect to have to deal with in the Lowcountry. Every few years Mother Nature decides to share some of the white stuff with Charleston. The first time I ever saw snow in Charleston, it was just some flurries—and it was a big deal. On the TV news that night, a reporter was broadcasting live from a covered gas station, and I vividly remember him shouting, "Look, that car still has snow on its roof!" If the forecast predicts anything more than just flurries, the supermarket shelves are stripped bare of bread, eggs, and milk, causing me to wonder if everyone rushes home to make French toast.

For years, any snow accumulation would easily melt by early the next morning. But in 2012, there was a snowstorm with enough snow that the roads were not clear the next day. It wasn't much snow, just a few inches, but there was ice involved, too. We sat at home and waited for the roads to be plowed so it would be safe to drive. (Not surprisingly, the drivers here aren't the best when it comes to snowy and icy roads.) No plows ever arrived, and we just had to wait for everything to melt. My son and I later saw our neighbor, Mayor Joe Riley (who kindly wrote the foreword to this book), and my son asked him why the streets hadn't been plowed, "The city doesn't own any plows," the mayor replied. There had never been enough snow to justify the expenditure. Having grown up in New York, I'd never even considered that.

The great thing about snow in Charleston is that its arrival is treated with such joy. If there is any accumulation at all, people flood into the streets, snowmen are built, and snow angels are made by kids wearing shorts. If it melts the next day, everyone is a little sad to see it go but so happy it came. If the snow lasts more than a day, it can cause some consternation because it does tend to get caught in your flip-flops.

On the Town

Many years ago, a friend told me that she loved living and working in downtown Charleston because there wasn't a week that went by when she didn't notice something new, whether that was an architectural detail or even a garden design she had never noticed before. The riches of Charleston are so numerous, they're hard to absorb in one look, in one week, in one year, perhaps in an entire lifetime.

I've always thought the best way to see Charleston is on foot. Whenever anyone asks me what they should do in Charleston, my answer is "Walk, walk, walk." (Next best is to take a carriage tour.) Not only does walking give you the chance to slow down and take in the details of what you are seeing, it gives you the chance to talk to the people you run across, peek through hedges and doors into gardens, and really get a sense of the neighborhoods. Walking the same street in one direction and then reversing course reveals a whole new set of beautiful sights. It's amazing what just a slight change in perspective can do.

Being out on the town also lets you take in more than just the architecture. The smells and sounds of Charleston add greatly to its charm and personality. Horses clopping by can take you back to an earlier time. Tour guides on passing carriages can be informative and entertaining. The pluff mud (rich sediment from the saltwater marshes) adds a distinctive Lowcountry fragrance to the air as you stroll along the water. Take a trip to the Charleston Farmers Market on Saturday mornings to experience delightful food, crafts, fresh veggies, and flowers. The same spot at night can feel totally different, more mysterious and beguiling.

Keep your eyes open for ghosts, too, as Charleston is one of the most haunted cities in the country. I had the pleasure of working in the Old City Jail, which is said to be the most haunted building in the city. Home to a number of well-known ghosts (including Lavinia Fisher, who is believed to be the first female mass murderer in the United States, and countless others), it's the setting for all sorts of otherworldly experiences. While many experiences were reported while I was there, from some very credible and seemingly sane people, the closest encounter I had with a ghost was when my pen cap became haunted (it's a long but good story). Our house used to have a ghost, too, but only our cats could see it (also another long but good story).

So, get out in Charleston. You never know what you'll find.

Sunrise, Sunset

Locals will tell you that the Cooper River, which runs down the east side of the Charleston peninsula, and the Ashley River, on the west, come together to form the mighty Atlantic Ocean. While that claim may be a bit ambitious, the rivers do merge to create Charleston Harbor, whose waters then form the Atlantic Ocean.

Okay, that might not be entirely true, either.

The fact is that Charlestonians are extremely proud of their city and sometimes may enhance the truth just a little bit. And if they do, it usually ends up being a pretty good story.

While those rivers may not be solely responsible for creating the world's second largest ocean, the Cooper and Ashley do provide the locations for the sun to have some spectacular rises and sets. Living downtown, a couple of blocks from the water, I've been lucky to have many opportunities to experience both. In the mornings, after dropping the kids off at school or on my way to work, I have the chance to see the sun's first rays spread across the harbor and the Cooper River, lighting up the wonderful houses along the High Battery, the beautiful Riley Waterfront Park, and the rest of the riverside that runs along the port to the Ravenel (Cooper River) Bridge.

After getting home in the evening and walking over to the Ashley (when the kids were little, we had a nightly tradition of throwing rocks in the water before dinner), the sun puts on a show on the western side of the peninsula as it casts its last light across the Ashley to the Low Battery, the river's marshes, Brittlebank Park, and the dramatic buildings of the Citadel (the Military College of South Carolina).

The evening show always draws more admirers (likely that has something to do with them already being out of bed). The colors are striking, and the breeze is usually refreshing. Early risers, however, can often catch crowds of ibis (yes, a flock of ibis is called a "crowd") heading across the harbor to find their breakfast in the marshes of James Island, pelicans scouting and plunging for fish, and dolphins breaking the surface of the water with an exhaled whoosh of air. As it goes down, the sun paints the sky, the ibis return home, the pelicans ride the final thermals of the day over the Fort Sumter House next to White Point Garden, and the dolphins swim by, making the incredible sunsets even more memorable.

Acknowledgments

The path to making a *Glimpses of Charleston* book a thrilling reality has been a winding one, full of much support and energy from quite a few people.

First, I am grateful to my family. Words cannot express how much I appreciate Kay, Morgan, and Ben, for their inspiration and love, as well as putting up with me whenever we were out and I said, "hold on, I have to take a picture." All the help and advice from my sister Sharon AvRutick, an editor extraordinaire, and my author brother-in-law, Joe Wallace, was invaluable. And I will always be so appreciative of my parents, Alice and Julian AvRutick, for a lifetime of unwavering support.

As a beneficiary of Mayor Joseph P. Riley Jr.'s forty years of extraordinary leadership, I am indebted to him for not only for writing the foreword to this book, but for the incredible vision, passion, and energy he brought to shaping Charleston and preserving its spectacular beauty. Even more, I am grateful to him for marrying me to Kay. I also appreciate that the Charleston RiverDogs, the NY Yankee's Class A baseball team for whom my son Ben works as their batboy, plays at "The Joe," which was named in honor of the mayor.

Thank you to Jonathan Poston whose incredible book, *The Buildings of Charleston*, from which I've learned so much of the built history of Charleston.

A huge thumbs up to the followers and fans of the Glimpses of Charleston Facebook page, where it all started. I so appreciate all your likes, great comments, words of support, sharing of the photos and putting up with my silly daily questions.

I've been very fortunate to work with Amy Lyons and the great team at Globe Pequot. Thanks for seeing the book in *Glimpses* and helping make this dream come true.

Finally, thank you to the City of Charleston, for being Charleston.

About the Author

While originally from "off," **David R. AvRutick** has been a full-time resident of downtown Charleston for almost twenty years, having been a part-time resident for the previous ten. As the founding president of the American College of the Building Arts–the only college of its kind in the United States–David led the creation of this unique Charleston institution which educates those who now help restore, maintain, and create lasting beauty in the structures of Charleston, the nation, and beyond. When not taking photographs, David is a serial entrepreneur (check out what Alice's Clubhouse is doing for families suffering with Alzheimer's and dementia) and lives two blocks from the Battery in downtown Charleston with his wife, two children, and their cats Max and Lola. You can reach David through the Glimpses of Charleston Facebook page or the *Glimpses of Charleston* website.

Shortly after the horrific shootings at the Mother Emanuel AME Church, Charlestonians came together after a Charleston RiverDogs baseball game to form a giant heart–showing that the beauty of Charleston is much more than skin deep.